What You Should Know About The United Nations

By

The League of Empire Loyalists

The A.K. Chesterton Trust

2012

First published by the League of Empire Loyalists in 1959.

This second edition is *The A.K. Chesterton Trust Reprint Series # 3*

Printed & Published 2012.

ISBN 978-0-9564669-4-5

© **The A.K. Chesterton Trust, BM Candour, London, WC1N 3XX, United Kingdom.**

Website: www.candour.org.uk

This booklet is dedicated to the memory of Lieut. Col. "Jock" Creagh-Scott, one of the earliest to pledge his support to *Candour* in 1953.

"Jock" Creagh Scott

Foreword

This booklet was originally published by The League of Empire Loyalists in 1959, and we are pleased to publish this second edition as part of *The A.K. Chesterton Trust Reprint Series*. In preparing it for publication, once again we note the accuracy of the forecasts. The writing was on the wall 50 years ago. If only Britain had heeded the warnings of what lay ahead on the road to World Government.

2013 will see the 60th anniversary of A.K.'s journal *Candour* and the 40th anniversary of A.K. Chesterton's death. We aim to produce further booklets to mark these milestones over the next few months.

Candour **is still in the fight. Are you?**

Colin Todd

The A.K. Chesterton Trust
July 2012

DID YOU KNOW:

1. That the foundations of the Charter of the United Nations were laid at the Conference of Foreign Secretaries at Moscow in 1943?

(*Whitaker's Almanack*, 1959.)

2. That the UN Charter was finally drawn up in 1944 at Dumbarton Oaks and San Francisco in 1945 by the American "Communist and intimate of an exotic Wall Street coterie," Alger Hiss, and the Russian-born Zionist, Leo Pasvolsky, who was Assistant U.S. Secretary of State from 1936-46?

(*Time Magazine,* 18th May, 1953; *American Mercury,* July, 1958, and July, 1959; *Candour—the British Views-Letter,* 22nd October, 1954)

(a) "Who were the principal movers at San Francisco for this United Nations Charter? Who wrote the charter, and who had the most to do about shaping its provisions? The answer is that the Russian Communists and Alger Hiss, a representative of our State Department, were the prime movers and schemers in arranging its provisions. That is the same Alger Hiss who was convicted of perjury when he denied sending secret material to the Soviet Union representatives. Its very beginning gave this document a bad odour."

(From a speech by Representative Usher Burdick in the House of Representatives, 28th April, 1954.)

3. That Pasvolsky copied whole sections of the UN Charter word for word, and virtually intact, from the Kremlin's dishonest "constitution of the U.S.S.R."?

(Commander Hilary Grey, R.N. (Retd.) in *American Mercury*, July, 1959.)

(a) "The (UN) Charter is in the main a translation of the Russian system into an international idiom and its adaptation to an international community... UNO bore upon its brow from the very beginning the mark of Moscow."

(From the book *Victors Beware!* by the Spanish Liberal, Professor S. D. Madariaga.)

(b) "Like the Communist Manifesto... the Charter of the United Nations is an evil imposture."

(Derek Tozer, M.A., in *Candour*, 22nd October, 1954.)

4. That the first Secretary-General of the United Nations Organisation was the conspirator Alger Hiss?

(The title in 1945 was The United Nations Conference On International Organisation.)

5. That the second Secretary-General, Mr. Trygve Lie, a Norwegian Socialist, was considered by the Comintern to be one of its chosen instruments?

(Leon Trotsky in his book *Stalin and his Crimes*.)

(a) "A Norwegian General Staff Intelligence Report, dated January 28, 1921, revealed that Trygve Lie had negotiated a secret agreement on behalf of the Norwegian Labour Party, pledging unconditional obedience to the Comintern in Moscow."

(Commander Hilary Grey, R.N. (retd.) in *American Mercury*, July, 1959.)

6. That the present Secretary-General, Dag Hammarsjkold, revealed his affinity for Red causes when in 1958 he dismissed the Dane, Mr. Povl Bang-Jensen, Deputy Secretary of the five-nation UN enquiry into the Hungarian rising of 1956, for refusing to hand over the names of the 81 Hungarian witnesses who had

given evidence only under promise of strict anonymity for fear of secret police reprisals against their relatives?

(a) "The Honorable Robert Morris, former Counsel of the Senate Internal Security Committee, charges that the United Nations dismissal of Povl Bang-Jensen was engineered by an international Communist conspiracy... The Bang-Jensen report delivered a devastating blow against Soviet reputation and caused defections in Communist parties throughout the world. Judge Morris says that the Communists have been conspiring to destroy Bang-Jensen on the theory that if you destroy the symbol, you destroy the effectiveness of the report... Judge Morris said Mr. Bang-Jensen's dismissal 'without the semblance of due process' is an outrage."

(J. Edward Johnston Jr. in *American Mercury*, February, 1958.)

7. That the Security Council, from the beginning, has always had a Communist Under-Secretary? (A.A. Sobelov (USSR), Constantin E. Zinchenko (USSR), Ilya S. Tcherynchev (USSR), Mr. Protitch (Yugoslavia) and Mr. Dragashav (Yugoslavia)

(The Secretary-General is ex-officio Secretary of the Security Council.)

(a) This means that the Communists, through their Under Secretary, have close touch with all military plans.

(Congressman Burdick in the House of Representatives on 17th January, 1957.)

(b) "On the Security Council his (the Secretary-General's) principal assistant has been for the past few years, Mr. Dragashav, a Yugoslav national. Under the recent reorganization of Secretariat functions, this post will be held by a Soviet national *as it has been previously*."

(Letter from a Congressman in reply to one of his constituents in July, 1958. The Congressman states that the answer was "prepared in collaboration with the Department of State.")

8. That the UN is impotent to defend rights?

(a) "I worked with the Security Council in New York from 1948 to 1951 and, in common with those who have first-hand knowledge, I know that so far as security is concerned it is impossible to rectify what Mr. Edwards euphemistically de-scribes as its (UNO's) 'deficiencies.' The failings are abysmal and fundamental. They spring from the false premise, underlying the security provisions of the United Nations Charter, that all the Great Powers have the security of the world at heart and will pull together honestly for it. But for 10 years it has been clear to all, save those who will not see, that Soviet Russia's aim is not security for all, but insecurity for the free world. That is the only climate in which Communism can germinate and flourish... So far as security is concerned, the United Nations is an instrument of proved efficiency for recording and eventually accepting *faits accomplis* but it is impotent to defend rights. Its troops are in the Suez area now only because British and French troops fought a way in for them."

(Air Marshal Sir Gerald Gibbs, in a letter to the *Daily Telegraph*, 20th December, 1956.)

(b) As long ago as 1950, when she was first invaded, Tibet complained to the UN Security Council. 'The Tibetans expressed the hope that 'the conscience of the world would not allow the disruption of our State by methods reminiscent of the jungle.' The appeal went on to say that 'If Tibet is compelled by force to become a part of China, against the will and consent of her people, the present invasion of Tibet will be the grossest instance of the violation of the weak by the strong...' But Tibet's appeal to the Security Council was in vain, and six months later (on May 27th, 1951), it was announced that an agreement for the 'peaceful liberation' of Tibet from 'imperialist influences' had been signed in Peking."

(*Common Cause Bulletin*, May, 1959.)

(c) To date (July, 1959) the UN has taken no action against the Chinese Communists for their barbarous invasion of Tibet. And now, nine years later, the Dalai Lama has made another appeal "to the conscience of the world" from his temporary refuge in India. He denounced not only the Chinese aggression but the continuing atrocities, and asserted that the ultimate aim of the Chinese was "near annihilation" of the Tibetan people. He stated that the number of Tibetans killed was even greater than that given recently by the international commission of jurists. He quoted 65,000 deaths as the figure since 1956 and said that the rate was very much higher since 1950. Over 1,000 monasteries had been destroyed, many lamas imprisoned and all places of worship closed. He spoke of deportations, imprisonment, interrogation and punishment without limit. He also stated that 9,000,000 Chinese colonisers were being settled in Tibet.

(Details taken from the *Daily Telegraph*, 22nd June, 1959.)

(d) "...the Assembly may prepare and adopt 'conventions' or 'declarations' which embody a code of proper behaviour by states; these it will ask states to ratify, passing the necessary domestic laws to give effect to them. In this last category come such instruments as the Convention on Genocide, which seeks to make group murder a crime (adopted by the Assembly in 1948) ..."

(H. G. Nicholas in *The United Nations As A Political Institution.*)

(e) "The Genocide Convention is NOT a treaty to protect human rights on a world-wide scale. Instead, it is a political shillelagh for the police state. The Article that forewarns us of this is Article II... This means that 'inhuman wrongs' can be committed against fellow human beings, so long as the wrongs are committed against those who are claimed to be "enemies of the State." Any dictator anywhere would enthusiastically support such a treaty provision."

(The Rev. Claude Bunzel in *American Mercury*, November, 1956.)

(f) The UN took no action against Soviet Russia in 1956 for her brutal aggression against Hungary, a (theoretically) independent sovereign State, nor for her earlier savage repressions in Eastern Germany and Poland.

(g) "The Genocide Convention has not been invoked for the race murder of 30,000,000 Greek Orthodox Christians in Soviet Russia and her 'captive nations.' Also it did not apply to the 800,000 Arabs during the Zionist rape of Arab Palestine."

(Cmdr. H. Grey, R.N., in *American Mercury*, July, 1959.)

(h) "Nearly 50,000,000 Christians disappeared from among the faithful during the recent revolutions in Eastern Europe.'

(Robert Tobias in *World Christian Digest*, August, 1957.)

(i) "In 1952 the Free Trade Union Committee of the AFL brought to the attention of the UN the appalling fact that Communists in occupied China had committed 14,000,000 political murders. The UN would take no action... In 1953 the United Nations Economic and Social Council was asked to discuss the use of slave labour in the Soviet Union. The council removed the item from its agenda. It would not discuss the matter. The slavery, as far as the UN was concerned, could continue."

(Karl Hess in *American Mercury*, March, 1956.)

9. That the UN is an instrument of international Communism and the power behind it, the international Money Power?

(a) "It is our conviction, based on long years of careful study, that world Zionism—fed by the illimitable wealth of the dominant New York Money Power—is the strongest of all the pressure-groups active in the field of international affairs. It played a decisive part in the financing of the Bolshevik Revolution. It used Roosevelt as a puppet to bring that Revolution into the heart of Europe. It created the United Nations and the various associate agencies, including the World Bank."

(A.K. Chesterton, M.C., in *Candour*, 16th November, 1956.)

(b) "Nasser's action in stealing the (Suez) Canal from its rightful owners, an international company, was quite indefensible on any grounds of legality or morality... It proved him to be a man unfit to be trusted with such a vital international waterway. Moreover there was ample reason to believe that he was receiving from the Soviet bloc supplies of arms far in excess of any conceivable requirements of the Egyptian armed forces themselves... Complete evacuation of Egyptian territory by British, French, and Israeli forces eventually took place under a barrage of United Nations admonitions, American economic pressure, bombastic Russian threats, hysterical abuse from left-wing and international schools of thought in the United Kingdom, and much uninformed criticism from all over the world."

(Major-General Richard Hilton, D.S.O., M.C., D.F.C., in *The Thirteenth Power*.)

(c) "The United States was involved in the Korean war and prevented from winning it by the United Nations. Communist China was advised before it entered the war that its own territory would be immune from attack... The vaunted authority of the UN is a myth attested by its failure to condemn Communist Russia, admittedly the master aggressor in Korea."

(Chesley Manly, in his book *The United Nations Record*.)

(d) We know how our policy was directed to let Korea fall, without letting it look as if we pushed her... We know now the victory was taken away from us, in the dark recesses of collaboration between our State Department and the United Nations."

(Senator William E. Jenner, in his farewell speech to the Senate at the end of 1958. Quoted from *Congressional Record*.)

(e) "We were required to lose the Korean war."

(Lieut.-General George Stratemeyer, USAF, in a speech on 25th August, 1954.)

(f) "General Ridgway told me in answer to my query as to why we can't win that he was *under orders not to win*."

(The American radio commentator, H. V. Kaltenborn, in a letter to the *Palm Beach Post*, 3oth January, 1952, and quoted in *The Iron Curtain Over America*, by Professor John Beaty.)

(g) "In each successive blow to British prestige in the Middle East, from Abadan to Suez, the hand of a great power can be seen to have worked against British interests... When it was not America herself who acted against the British, this job was taken over by the United Nations. Both America and the United Nations are, as we have seen, tools of the New York money power, and the implements of its global policy."

(Major-General Richard Hilton, D.S.O., M.C., D.F.C., in his book *The Thirteenth Power*.)

10. That the UN seeks to impose "Universal Brotherhood" and "Peace" by means of World Dictatorship?

(a) "There is, I think, little doubt that the majority of members of the World Government organisations such as the *World Movement for World Federal Government*, the *Commonwealth of World Citizens*, the *United Nations Association*, and the *World Association of Parliamentarians for World Government*, are well-meaning people, genuinely anxious to further the cause of international goodwill. However impatient we become with their political innocence we must not forget that. We do not scoff at their desire for peace (though we point out that there are things which should be dearer to a Christian), but we must dispel the naïveté which allows them to believe that the road they are travelling will take them to a world acceptable to Christians—or even to a world in which Christians will be tolerated."

(Aidan Mackey in *Candour*, 10th December, 1954.)

(b) "Even while the war was still being waged the policy-makers of New York, using as tools Red agents such as Alger Hiss and Harry Dexter White, brought into being the United Nations as the basis of a projected super-state and the World Bank as the basis of a projected international credit monopoly."

(A.K. Chesterton, M.C., in his booklet *Sound The Alarm*.)

(c) "I and my friends are convinced that the power of Britain is being fatally undermined by a false theory—that sovereignty can be submerged in some predicated system of international justice or morality, into some political organisation called the United Nations or NATO or something else. We are becoming convinced... that American liberalism... is remorselessly depriving us of our independence, manoeuvring against our Empire and against our points of military strength overseas, and at this moment, in NATO, is hauling us on board a juggernaut in Europe which it has created and against an enemy of its own choice."

(Lord Hinchinbrooke in a speech during a Foreign Affairs debate in the House of Commons in December, 1957.)

(d) "The stranglehold of international finance is not just the plaything of one rich man. It is the corporate possession of an oligarchy, whose headquarters is in New York, but whose true nationality is no more American than Chinese. It is an oligarchy without real bonds of loyalty to any nation... Russia with her Communism, is cunningly being utilized as the two shots of the ambush (i.e., in the dual capacity of war-machine and purveyor of subversion.) America, perhaps entirely against the wishes of most Americans, is being used by the international money power as the weapon with which the free world is to be forced into 'one-world Government'."

(Major-General Richard Hilton, D.S.O., M.C., D.F.C., in his book *The Thirteenth Power*.)

(e) "World Government involves the surrender to an international police force of all national arms. It is an attractive case to argue before the bulk of electors, in as far as most people are politically superficial, and in as far as their ignorance nowadays is often accompanied by atrophied instincts. That is why it is so dangerous... As the inhabitants of the United Kingdom are outnumbered four to one by the inhabitants of the Soviet Union, and twelve to one, or thereabouts, by the inhabitants of Red China, some allowance should be made for the likelihood that the international police would look more like Mongols than like Cockneys, and that the standards of decency and fair play which they imposed might well be Russian and Chinese rather than British."

(A.K. Chesterton, M.C., in his booklet *The Menace of World Government*.)

(f) "Her Majesty's Government are fully in agreement with world government. We agree that this must be the goal, and that every step that is humanly possible must be taken to reach that goal... Surely, the Declaration of Common Purpose is a step in that direction.. To use the United Nations machinery for world government is, again, obviously a goal.

(Lord Gosford, in a speech for the Government in the House of Lords, *Hansard*, 7th Nov., 1957, Column 192.)

(g) "If once the great Powers could agree to disarm and to set up a system of international control, we should have gone a good way along the road, which I hope will lead us eventually to *the establishment of a world authority with a world police force... I believe that, in the long run, nothing short of that will really work.*"

(Mr. Duncan Sandys, Minister of Defence, in a speech during the Conservative Party Conference at Brighton in October, 1957.)

(h) "... in the near future... the nations of the free world must make an even more significant contribution of their national sovereignty to the common cause than hitherto."

(Mr. Harold Macmillan, Prime Minister, in a speech in the House of Commons. *Hansard*, 5th November, 1957, Vol. 577. Column 39.)

(i) "We are anxious to know what the Prime Minister meant in another place on Tuesday when he spoke of NATO and the nations of the free world making an even more significant contribution of their national sovereignty... We are anxious because we are not quite sure what effect *the surrender of sovereignty* would have on our Commonwealth partners, and I think we should be told."

(Lord Ogmore in the House of Lords, 7th November, 1957. *Hansard*, Vol. 206, Column 134.)

(j) "As it stands, I think this is a revolutionary statement (i.e., the above statement by the Prime Minister.) I am one of those who value national sovereignty. I value it as an English Member of the British Parliament in allegiance to Crown and country. I value it as a citizen of the Commonwealth, which is built on national sovereignty... I believe that nationhood must be the starting point for European unity... But I am convinced that national sovereignty must be maintained and the essential weapons kept in national hands."

(Mr. John Biggs-Davison, M.P., in the House of Commons, 8th November, 1957. *Hansard*, Columns 537 and 538.)

(k) "What the Government is moving toward is as plain as it is perilous. Our present destiny—a satellite state in the universal Soviet dictatorship—is nothing less than a centralized world government, and the short cut we are taking toward it is through the United Nations. *The world government threat is seldom discussed in print.* Even when the threat is discussed in the halls of Congress, the newspapers are strangely silent."

(Russell Maguire, Chairman of the Board of *American Mercury*, in editorial reprints, January to June, 1955.)

11. That the UN brainwashes children of the free world?

(a) "There was evidence that UNESCO (United Nations Educational, Scientific and Cultural Organisation) was brainwashing patriotism out of our youngsters and substituting the United Nations for God..."

(Paul Harvey in *American Mercury*, July, 1958.)

(b) "Love of country is particularly and specifically discouraged in a UNESCO publication entitled *Principles of Social Reconstruction*. It condemns 'bigoted nationalism' in history books. A sequel to it regards *any* degree of nationalism as undesirable."

(Karl Hess in *American Mercury*, March, 1956.)

(c) "If we could effectively kill the national pride and patriotism of just one generation we have won that country. Therefore there must be continual propaganda abroad to undermine the loyalty of the citizens in general and the teenager in particular."

(From the book *Brain-Washing. A Synthesis of The Communist Textbook on Psychopolitics*, published by The Victorian League of Rights, Melbourne, Australia.)

(d) "The formation of the one-world mentality cannot be achieved while local loyalties remain paramount. Regardless of the sophistries uttered by her Director-General, UNESCO's hatred of national sovereignty is manifest. It is, of course, the child who is first infected with its virus. 'As long as the child breathes the poisoned air of nationalism, education in world-mindedness can produce only precarious results. As we have pointed out, it is frequently the family that infects the child with extreme nationalism.' (*In the Classroom with Children under 13 years of age*, UNESCO official publication). So love of Queen and country, even family, must be countered at the very earliest stage. It is the vital role of the kindergarten or nursery school to combat the 'outgrowth of the narrow family spirit'."

(Derek Tozer, M.A., in *Candour*, 30th July/6th August, 1954.

(e) "This English One Worlder and idol of UNESCO (Bertrand Russell) makes it clear in his latest book, *The Impact of Science on Society*, that he regards any degree of nationalism as a manifestation of bigotry... Here is a glimpse of One World, as conceived by Lord Russell, a self-styled 'democratic Socialist' :

"It is to be expected that advances in physiology and psychology will give governments much more control over individual mentality than they now have even in totalitarian countries... Diet, injections, and injunctions will combine, from a very early age, to produce the sort of character and the sort of beliefs that the

authorities consider desirable, and any serious criticisms of the powers that be will become psychologically impossible. Even if all are miserable, all will believe themselves happy because the government will tell them that they are so."

(Chesley Manly in *American Mercury*, June, 1953.)

(f) "Now we in British medicine are trying to learn all we can about these terrible and most effective methods of changing men's thoughts and beliefs on a large scale, because I believe ultimately the fate of the world will depend on the conversion of the masses to one idea of life or another."

(Dr. Sargent in a talk on the B.B.C. on November 11th, 1953.)

(g) "But it is in agencies like the World Health Organisation and UNESCO that we find alarming evidence of the insidious attack upon the mind by men who make it clear that they are determined to destroy Christian civilization. The writers of the textbook on psychopolitics must warmly applaud the following statement by Dr. Brock Chisholm, Director of the World Health Organisation: 'We have swallowed all manner of poisonous certainties fed us by our parents, our Sunday and day school teachers.' And how does Dr. Chisholm propose to rectify this: 'Reinterpretation and eventually eradication of the concept of right and wrong... Most psychiatrists and psychologists have escaped from these moral chains.'... The daily press tells him (the average individual) little or nothing of such conferences as the International Congress on Mental Health held in 1948. Dr. Chisholm presided, and speaker after speaker spoke of the necessity of 'mental healing' to break down the ties of family, nation, and religion."

(Eric D. Butler, Director, Victorian League of Rights, 1956 in his Introduction to the book *Brain-Washing. A Synthesis of the Communist Textbook on Psychopolitics*.)

12. That the UN harbours Communist spies?

(a) "Use of the UN as a cover for Soviet espionage operations has been spotlighted in U.S. Congressional investigations. More than 40 American members of the UN Secretariat were dismissed because of possible connections with the Communist Party. Two hundred persons resigned without explanation during the investigations."

(Karl Hess in *American Mercury*, March, 1956.)

(b) "A United States Senate spot-check in January, 1951, found that 32 per cent of UN representatives from foreign countries were trained Communist spies and that 29 per cent were actually under surveillance by the F.B.I... In December, 1952 an American Federal Grand Jury found that 'an overwhelmingly large group of disloyal United States citizens [are employed by the United Nations... in key positions,] and that 'almost without exception' these Communist sympathizers had previously been employed in the Truman Administration until exposed by Senators McCarthy, McCarran and other investigating Committees. Then they were speedily moved into well-paid, tax-exempt posts in the UN.

(Reported in the London *Daily Telegraph*, December 3, 1952)." (Commander Hilary Grey, R.N., in *American Mercury*, July 1959.)

(c) "Now trained espionage agents, operating under diplomatic immunity, could direct operations. After World War II Russians assigned to the United Nations in this country gave additional striking power to Soviet espionage. Moreover, assistance was possible through the espionage networks of Soviet satellite countries operating in the United States."

(J. Edgar Hoover, Director of the Federal Bureau of Investigation, in his book *Masters of Deceit*.)

13. That religion is threatened by the UN?

(a) The UN specifically asserts that religious freedom may be curbed by governments. Article 15 of the UN Covenant of Human Rights, section 3, says: "Freedom to manifest one's religion or beliefs may be subject only to such limitations as are prescribed by law..."

(b) "Rather than 'offend' any of its members, such as the atheists of the Soviet Union, the UN omits God from its considerations. And when UNESCO put up a $600,000 fund to underwrite a new world history, it chose as editor Professor Ralph Turner of Yale, described in William F. Buckley's *God and Man at Yale* as a 'dedicated iconoclast who has little mercy for God, or on those who believe in Him.'"

(Karl Hess in *American Mercury*, March, 1956.)

(c) "An excellent example of that thought appears in the booklet *UNESCO, Its Purpose and Philosophy*, which Huxley wrote as Director-General of UNESCO... After destroying, to his own satisfaction, the certitudes of Christianity, he assures his readers that 'Science... on the basis of its fruitful experience, asserts with confidence that... truth is never complete and explanation never fully or eternally valid.' But, a little later, having disposed of superstition, he proudly proclaims that Science 'produces an ever-increasing body of tested knowledge which is permanent and irrefutable.' If that appears to be somewhat self-contradictory, it is merely because the rarefied heights of the New Scientific Thought are not to be scaled by ordinary mortals. It is sufficient that science has spoken."

(Aidan Mackey, in *Candour*, 16th September, 1955.)

(d) "We emphatically oppose the United Nations because of its origin, for it was conceived in iniquity, born in corruption, and has been perpetuated on our soil with deceit and hypocrisy. The United Nations was formed to take the place of the League of Nations. Both were lifted directly from the Communist Manifesto; and both are merely an extension of World Revolution, which was to be the prelude to World Government... The United Nations Charter was written by such men as Dr. Leo Pasvolsky and Alger Hiss. Many of the Articles were lifted from the Constitution of the USSR. In it, all reference to man's dependence on God has been omitted... This omission was not accidental. It was planned that way to please the anti-Christs in Moscow and their dupes elsewhere. The UN is divided between Christians and atheists; therefore, it cannot and will not stand."

(Rev. J. A. Lovell, D.D., distinguished lecturer and broadcaster, in *American Mercury*, August, 1959.)

(e) "The adherence of Christian Churches to United Nations amounts to acceptance of a silent partnership in an anti-Christ militant movement. In their eager searching for a spiritual solution for recurring world wars they were deluded into embracing the fantasy of United Nations as the solution of the problem. But world-peace can never thrive or survive in United Nations because the spirit of Christ is completely absent. That creates insurmountable obstacles."

"Christian Churches, and their spiritual helmsmen, must now realize that United Nations has become an instrument for the application of force by the stronger against the weaker nations. United Nations has become a provoker of wars."

(Congressman John T. Wood (Idaho) in the House of Representatives, February 25th, 1952.)

14. That the UN flag takes precedence over the Union Jack—and all other national flags?

(a) "The deplorable custom has grown up in recent years of flying the UN flag on town halls, etc., on United Nations day. It is not generally known that one of the conditions attaching to the flying of this flag is that no other flag shall fly higher or be larger in size. In other words, it must take precedence over our National Flag. This claim ought to be repudiated at once by every Council which has had the habit of countenancing the flying of the flag. Let us not forget the behaviour of the United Nations over Suez, and their very different reactions to the Hungarian tragedy. It was the United Nations which rejected the Royal Navy's assistance in clearing the Suez Canal. It was the United Nations which insisted that the British ships should haul down the Ensign, that naval personnel should wear civilian clothes, and THEN, after inflicting this humiliation, failed to make use of them properly."

(Leslie Greene, M.A., Organising Secretary, The League of Empire Loyalists, in its *Bulletin* No. 18, 20th August, 1957.)

(b) "The following report, from the *B'nai B'rith News* of October, 1950, shows the kind of influence which has been at work to secure the flying of this emblem. B'nai B'rith, of course, is the notorious Jewish Secret Society. Pale blue and white, colours of the UN flag, are also the Jewish colours.

'Washington, D.C.—United Nations flags will be presented to the mayors of several leading cities throughout the world at public ceremonies on UN Day, October 24, as part of an international goodwill project sponsored by B'nai B'rith. 'President Frank Goldman conceived the international flag idea for B'nai B'rith stimulation and promotion in the foreign countries where lodges are located'..."

(From *Candour*, 4th November, 1955.)

15. That the UN threatens the freedom of the individual?

(a) "Interference in the home life of individual families is a stated UN purpose. In the UNESCO school programme's statements of intent, there is the declaration that UNESCO will try to 'correct many of the errors of home training... the narrow family spirit of the parents may, in fact, not only compromise indirectly, and in some degree unconsciously, the eventual integration of the child in the human community, but it may also cultivate attitudes running directly counter to the development of international understanding .. .

"Dean Acheson, former Secretary of State, has made it clear that the scope of the UN is not limited to discussions of national and international matters at a governmental level. The UN, he said, 'amounts to an international legislative system' that is empowered to 'deal with the individual and the rights of the individual' in any nation belonging to the UN."

(Karl Hess in *American Mercury*, March, 1956.)

(b) "The logic of the situation is unbeatable. Since an entirely new code of international law is being created to cope with a new catalogue of 'international crimes,' they must have a new court to try the new company of 'international criminals'... If you were to read the 55 articles of the draft statutes of this proposed International Criminal Court, you would likely come to this conclusion : Here is the draft for an international criminal court, with power to arrest *any individual for any crime* (assuming the State in question has granted jurisdiction, and the crime in question has been covered by some treaty)."

(Rev. Claude Bunzel, in *American Mercury*, November, 1956.)

CONCLUSION

"The UN should be appraised accurately for what it is: only the trap-door to Stalin's jail, baited with the Dove of Peace."

(Mr. Glenn O. Young, American lawyer and elder of the Presbyterian Church, recorded in *American Mercury*. July, 1959.)

JOIN THE LEAGUE OF EMPIRE LOYALISTS AND FIGHT FOR CHRISTIAN VALUES, BRITISH INDEPENDENCE AND INDIVIDUAL FREEDOM

As this booklet goes to press[1], there comes news of what is alleged to be the "suicide" of Mr. Povl Bang-Jensen, whose steadfast refusal to betray the identity of Hungarian witnesses who gave evidence about the Hungarian uprising of 1956 led to his dismissal by Mr. Dag Hammarsjkold (see section 6) After Mr. Bang-Jensen's disappearance, and before his body was discovered, the "Daily Telegraph" stated: "His friends are reported to believe that he may have been kidnapped by Communist agents, and may even be liquidated."

---

[1] Povl Bang-Jensen (6 April 1909 – 25 November 1959) was a Danish diplomat who refused to hand over a list of witnesses to the Hungarian Revolution of 1956 to his UN superiors, because he considered that if their identities were turned over to the UN Secretariat they would be leaked to the Russians, and reprisals would be taken against relatives in Hungary. He was found dead of a gunshot wound with the gun in his hand and suicide note in his pocket in Queens, New York City park on 26 November 1959.

WHAT YOU SHOULD KNOW ABOUT THE UNITED NATIONS

Do you value your religion?

Do you value your national independence?

Do you value your personal freedom?

Do you value the system of justice in your own country?

Do you value your national flag as a symbol of these things?

Do you want your children to be brought up to love and respect these things?

IF SO, READ THIS BOOKLET, FOR ALL ARE THREATENED BY THE UNITED NATIONS.

Issued by the

LEAGUE OF EMPIRE LOYALISTS

Price: One Shilling

The front cover of the 1959 first edition of this booklet

JOIN THE LEAGUE OF
EMPIRE LOYALISTS

The back cover of the 1959 first edition of this booklet

About A.K. Chesterton

Arthur Kenneth Chesterton was born at the Luipaards Vlei gold mine, Krugersdorp, South Africa where his father was an official in 1899.

In 1915 unhappy at school in England A.K. returned to South Africa. There and without the knowledge of his parents, and having exaggerated his age by four years, he enlisted in the 5th South African Infantry.

Before his 17th birthday he had been in the thick of three battles in German East Africa. Later in the war he transferred as a commissioned officer to the Royal Fusiliers and served for the rest of the war on the Western Front being awarded the Military Cross in 1918 for conspicuous gallantry.

Between the wars A.K. first prospected for diamonds before becoming a journalist first in South Africa and then England. Alarmed at the economic chaos threatening Britain, he joined Sir Oswald Mosley in the B.U.F and became prominent in the movement. In 1938, he quarrelled with Mosley's policies and left the movement.

When the Second World War started he rejoined the army, volunteered for tropical service and went through all the hardships of the great push up from Kenya across the wilds of Jubaland through the desert of the Ogaden and into the remotest parts of Somalia. He was afterwards sent down the coast to join the Somaliland Camel Corps and intervene in the inter-tribal warfare among the Somalis.

In 1943 his health broke down and he was invalided out of the army with malaria and colitis, returning to journalism. In 1944, he became deputy editor and chief leader writer of *Truth*.

In the early 1950s A.K. established *Candour* and founded the League of Empire Loyalists which for some years made many colourful headlines in the press worldwide. He later took that organisation into The National Front, and served as its Chairman for a time.

A.K. Chesterton died in 1973.

A.K. Chesterton

About The A.K. Chesterton Trust

The A.K. Chesterton Trust was formed by Colin Todd and the late Miss. Rosine de Bounevialle in January 1996 to succeed and continue the work of the now defunct Candour Publishing Co.

The objects of the Trust are stated as follows:

"To promote and expound the principles of A.K. Chesterton which are defined as being to demonstrate the power of, and to combat the power of International Finance, and to promote the National Sovereignty of the British World."

Our aims include:

- *Maintaining and expanding the range of material relevant to A.K. Chesterton and his associates throughout his life.*

- *To preserve and keep in-print important works on British Nationalism in order to educate the current generation of our people.*

- *The maintenance and recovery of the sovereign independence of the British Peoples throughout the world.*

- *The strengthening of the spiritual and material bonds between the British Peoples throughout the world.*

- *The resurgence at home and abroad of the British spirit.*

We will raise funds by way of merchandising and donations.

We ask that our friends make provision for *The A.K. Chesterton Trust* in their will.

The A.K. Chesterton Trust has a **<u>duty</u>** to keep *Candour* in the ring and punching.

CANDOUR: To defend national sovereignty against the menace of international finance.

CANDOUR: To serve as a link between Britons all over the world in protest against the surrender of their world heritage.

Subscribe to Candour

CANDOUR SUBSCRIPTION RATES FOR 10 ISSUES.

U.K. £25.00
Europe 40 Euros.
Rest of the World £35.00.
USA $50.00.

All Airmail. Cheques and Postal Orders, £'s Sterling only, made payable to *The A.K. Chesterton Trust*. (Others, please send cash by **secure post**, $ bills or Euro notes.)

Payment by Paypal is available. Please see our website **www.candour.org.uk** for more information.

Candour Back Issues

Back issues are available. 1953 to the present.

Please request our back issue catalogue by sending your name and address with two 1st class stamps to:

The A.K. Chesterton Trust, BM Candour, London, WC1N 3XX, United Kingdom.

Alternatively, see our website at **www.candour.org.uk** where you can order a growing selection on-line.

The A.K. *Chesterton Trust* Reprint Series

1. Creed of a Fascist Revolutionary & Why I Left Mosley - A.K. Chesterton.

2. The Menace of World Government & Britain's Graveyard - A.K. Chesterton.

3. What You Should Know About The United Nations - The League of Empire Loyalists.

4. The Menace of the Money-Power - A.K. Chesterton.

5. The Case for Economic Nationalism - John Tyndall.

6. Sound the Alarm! - A.K. Chesterton.

7. Six Principles of British Nationalism - John Tyndall.

8. B.B.C. - A National Menace - A.K. Chesterton.

9. Stand by the Empire - A.K. Chesterton.

10. Tomorrow. A Plan for the British Future - A.K. Chesterton

Other Titles from *The A.K. Chesterton Trust*

Leopard Valley - A.K. Chesterton.

Juma The Great - A.K. Chesterton.

The New Unhappy Lords - A.K. Chesterton.

Facing The Abyss - A.K. Chesterton.

The History of the League of Empire Loyalists - H. McNeile & R. Black

All the above titles are available from The A.K. Chesterton Trust, BM Candour, London, WC1N 3XX, UK

www.candour.org.uk

Printed in Poland
by Amazon Fulfillment
Poland Sp. z o.o., Wrocław